Dufy's Cat

Mary Moffitt Aycock

Dufy's Cat

Dufy's cat
who was fat
sat
on a rug
snug as a bug
in a room
all a'bloom
with colors
galore
on ceilings
and
floors
on the wall
in the hall
in yellow and mauve
(so fabulously fauve!)
and his cat
it would seem
was part of the
scene
for he was
lime green!

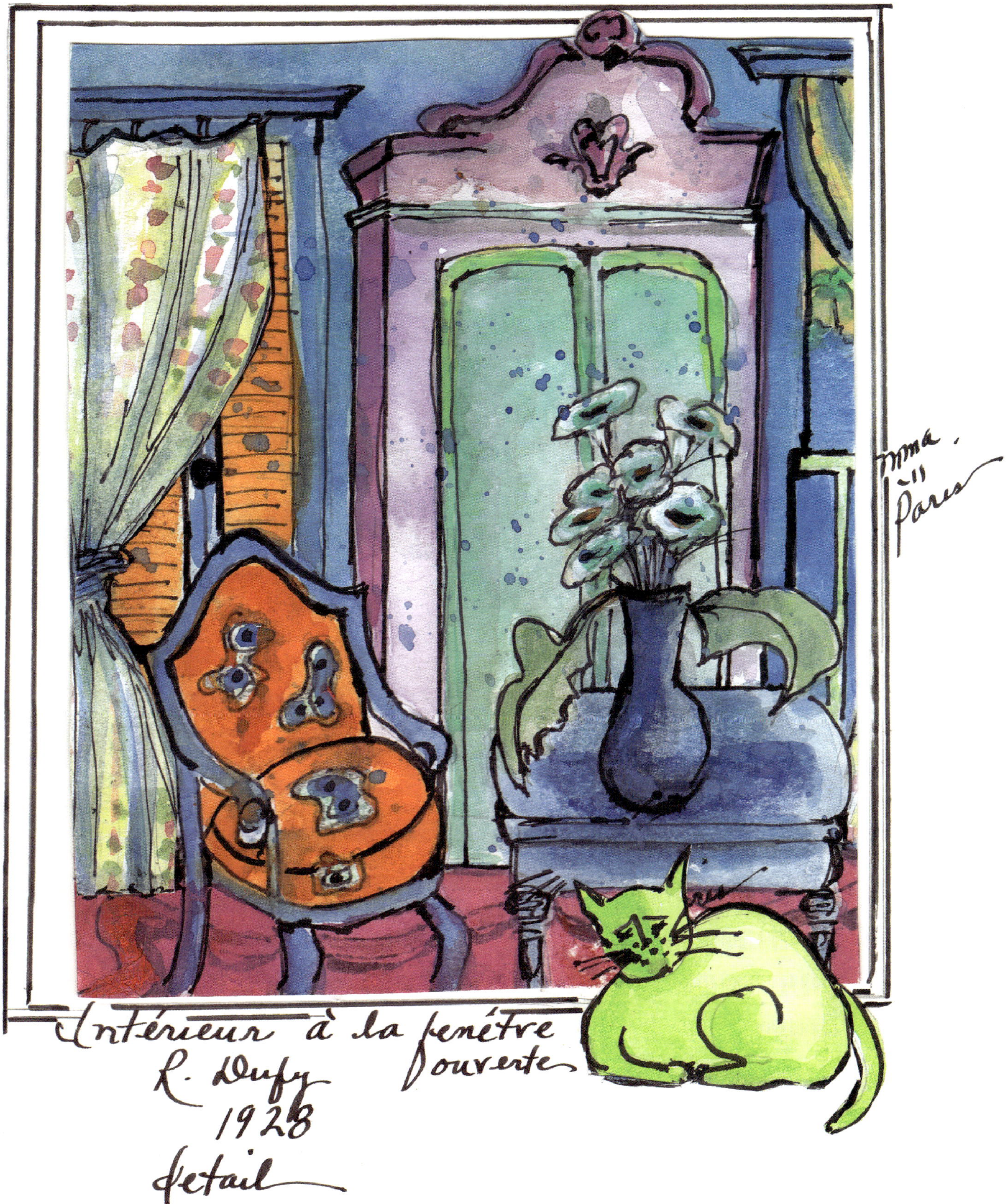

Intérieur à la fenêtre ouverte
R. Dufy
1928
detail

Henri's Cat

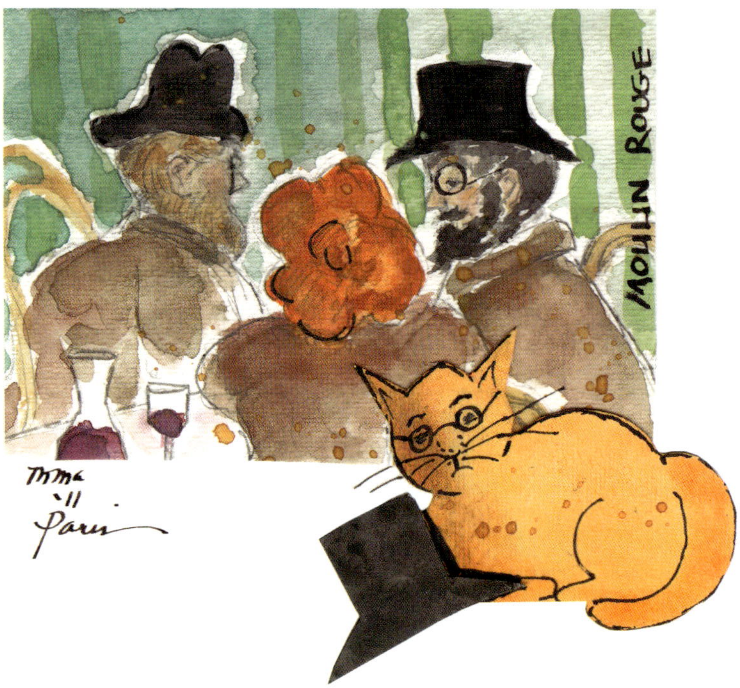

Toulouse - Lautrec
had a
defect
He wasn't tall
at all
in fact
he was small
And so was his
cat
who wore a top hat
when he sat
in cafés
or
cabarets
where men in
berets
watched
girls in pearls
twirl and swirl
with flaunts
and flirts
as they kicked up
their skirts
and Toulouse
cruised
and mused
which girl
to chose at
the
Moulin Rouge

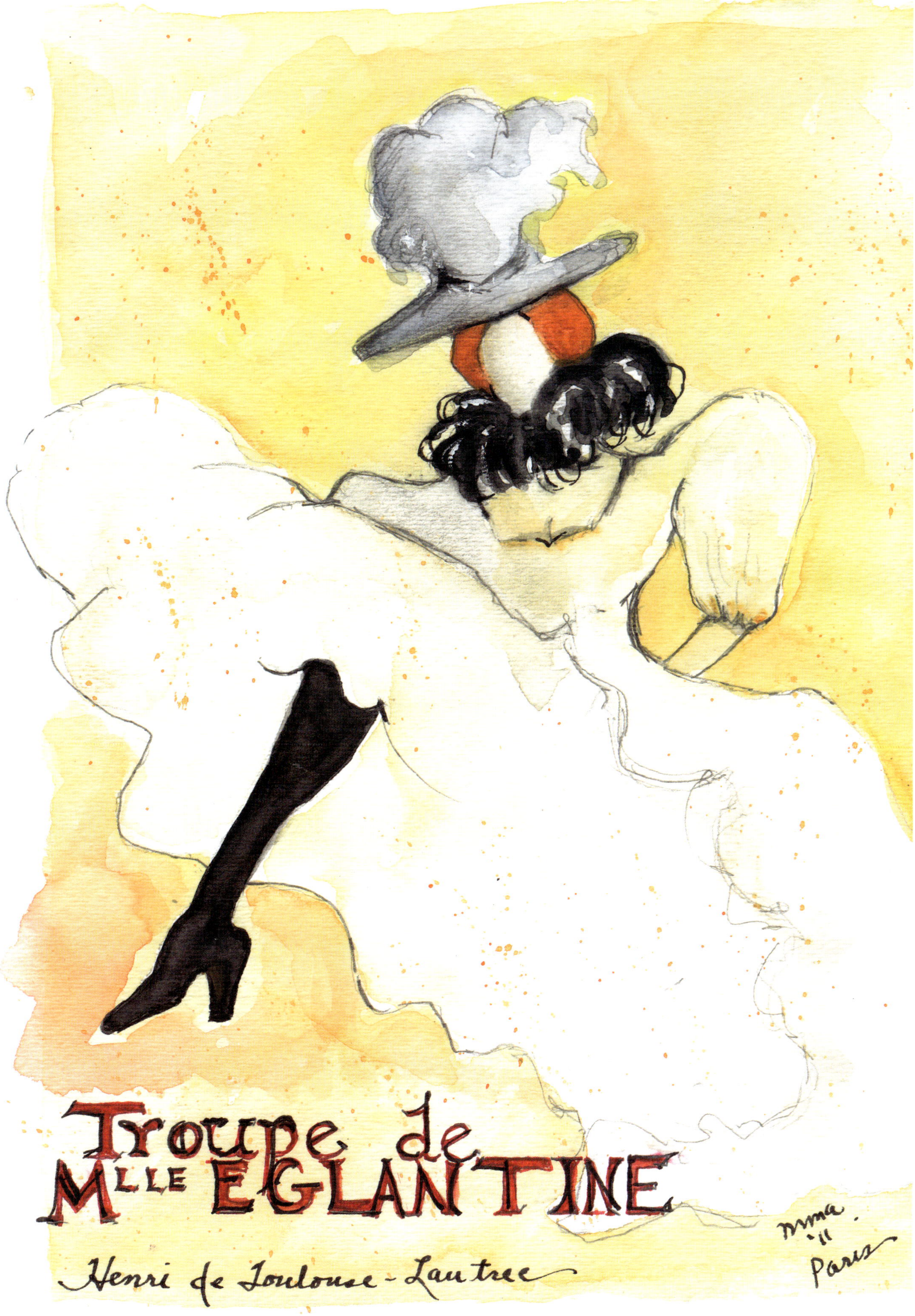
Troupe de
Mlle EGLANTINE
Henri de Toulouse-Lautrec
Paris

Pablo's Cat

Pablo's cat
was flat
but
four dimensional
and sensual
and he played
the guitar
in the Spanish War
in hues
of blues
of every kind
with Gertrude Stein
merging
space and time
He was made
of cubes
and tubes
a broken
token
of the human
schism
in syncopated rhythm

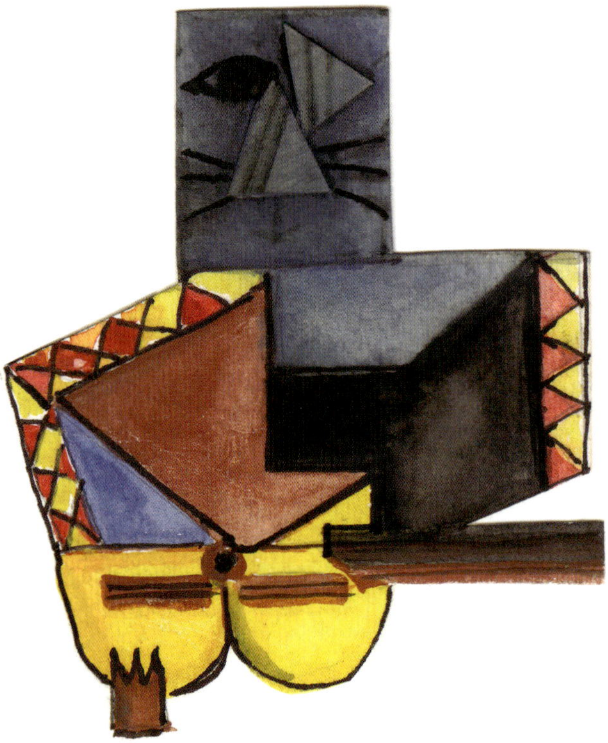

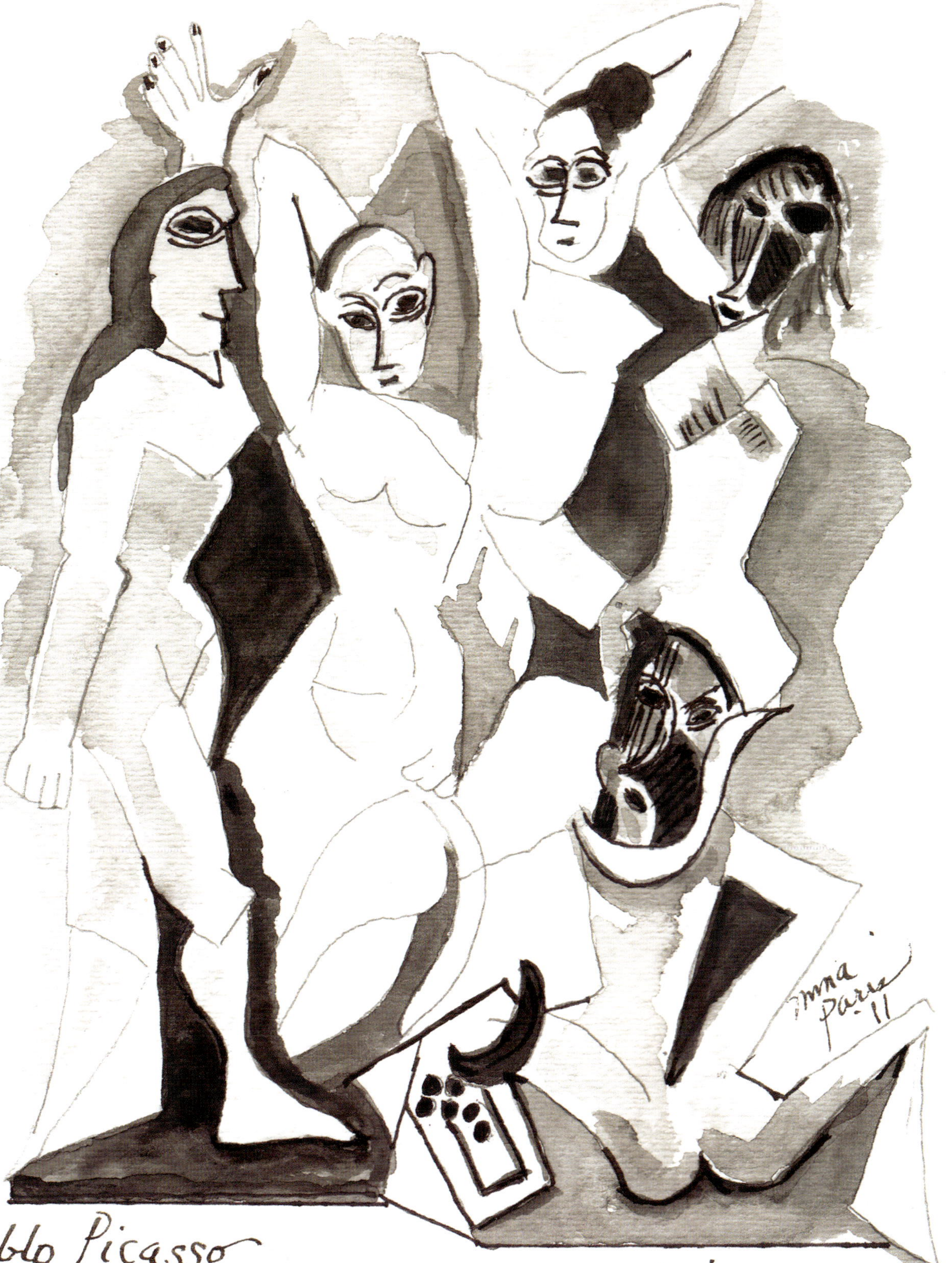

Pablo Picasso

detail
Les Desmoiselles
d'Avignon 1907

Matisse's Cat

The cat of Matisse
was a
little
wild beast
dense
intense
a lyrical flow
of
colors that
glow
with a vibrant
gleam
and a primitive
theme
Sometimes she
dined
sometimes reclined
in a
collage of color
a
collage of form
a joyous expression
of the
still
and the storm

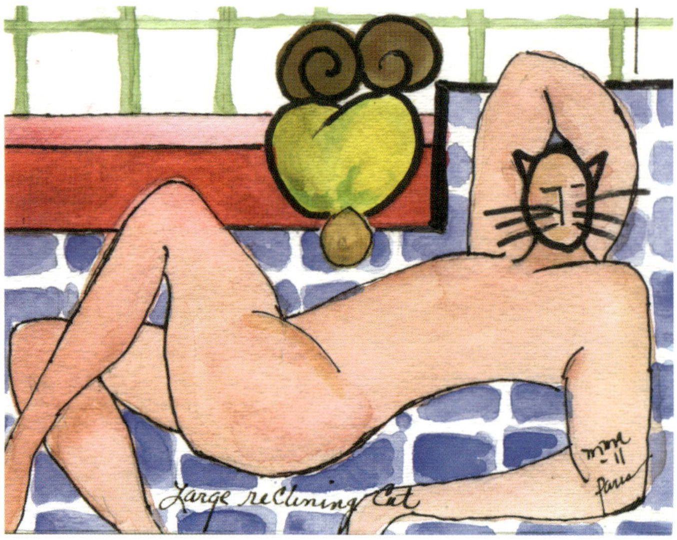

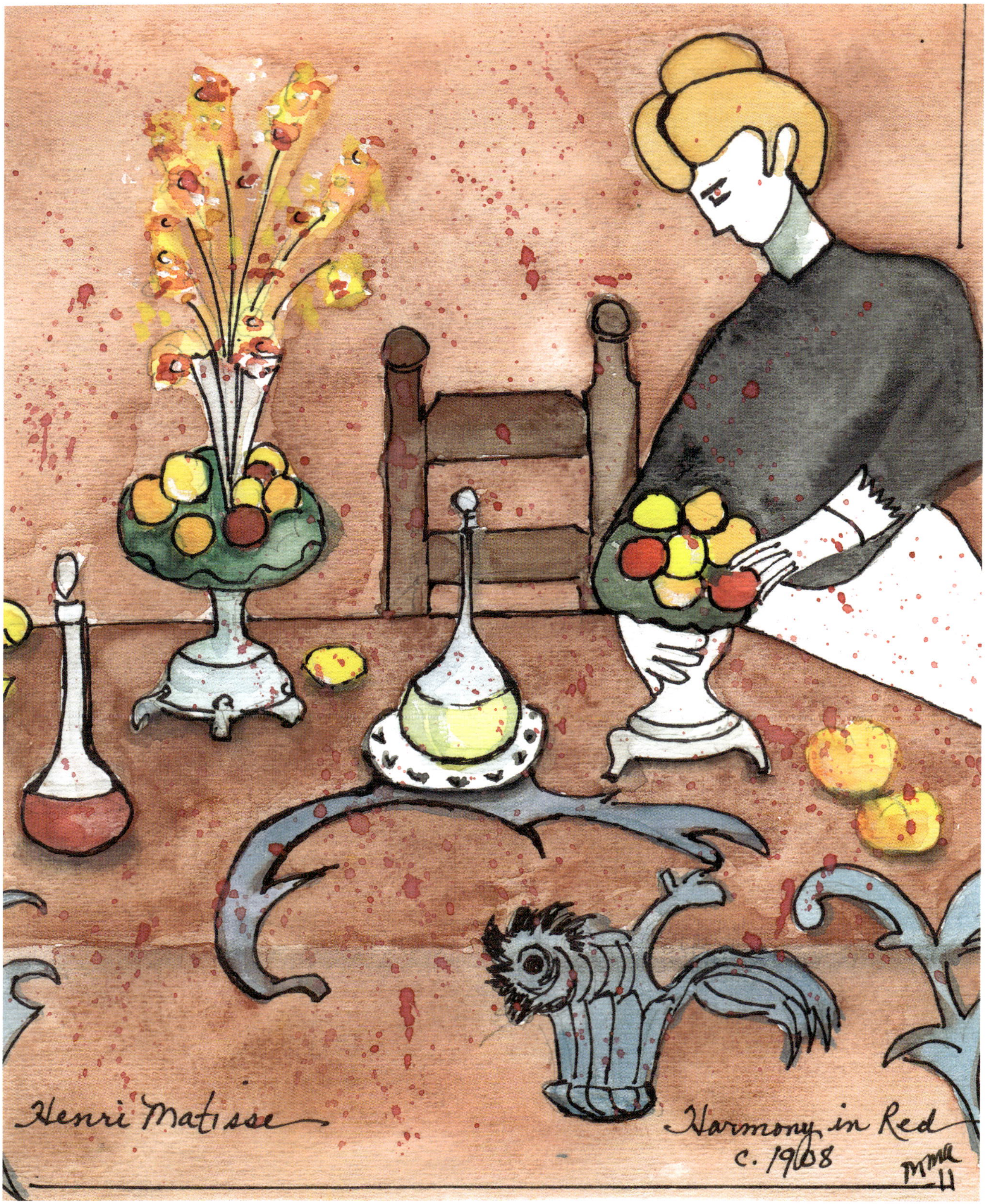
Henri Matisse
Harmony in Red
c. 1908

Modigliani's Cat

Modigliani
had a cat
named
Giani
with a heck
of a
neck
and a face
with the
grace
of a zulu
mask
cast
in the past
for a tribal
dance
long
strong
erotic
with the glint
of a hint
of
exotic
romance

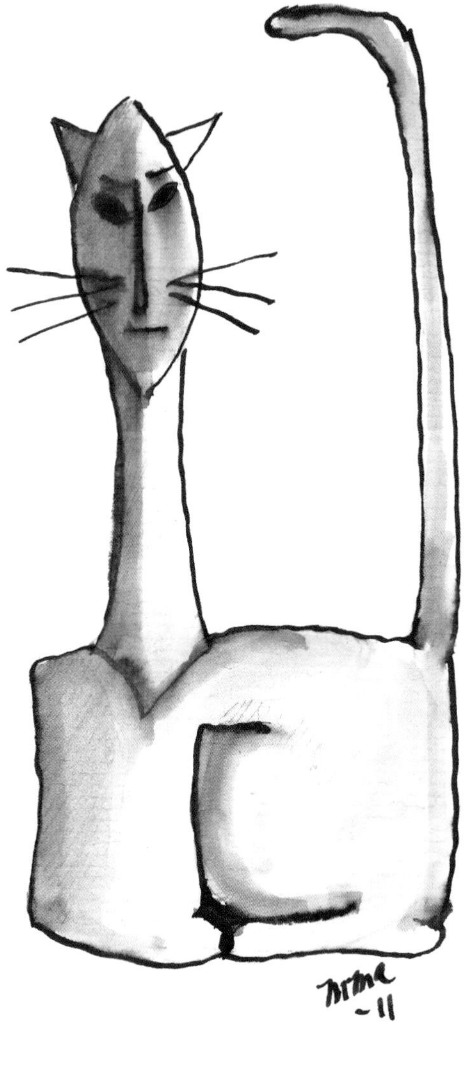

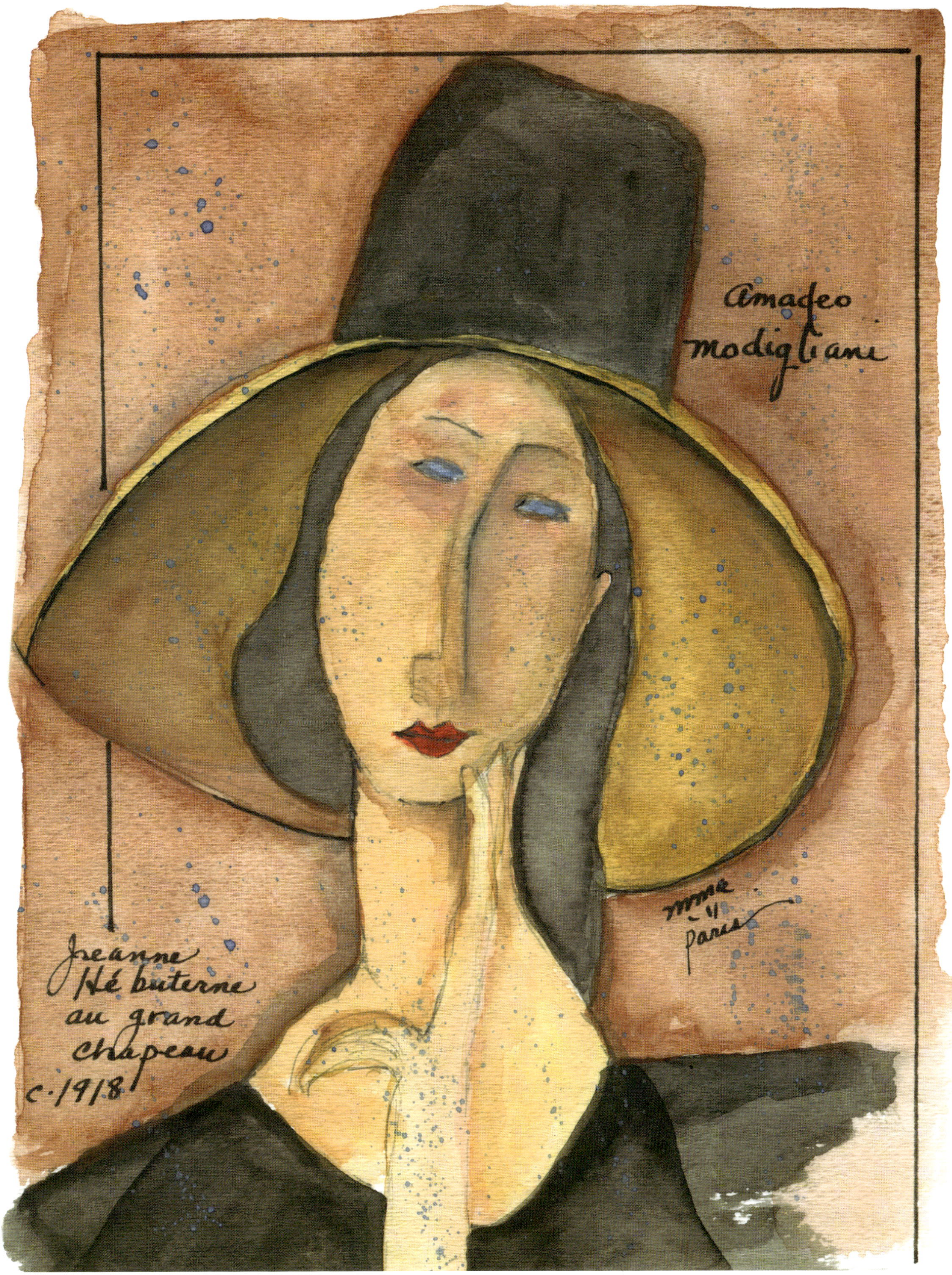
Amadeo
modigliani
Jeanne
Hébuterne
au grand
chapeau
c. 1918

Van Gogh's Cat

Van Gogh's cat
had one
ear
But he could hear
the music
of a starry night
And the dreary tune
of a saloon
in gaudy
light
And he could see
the grace
of yellow flowers
in a
yellow
vase

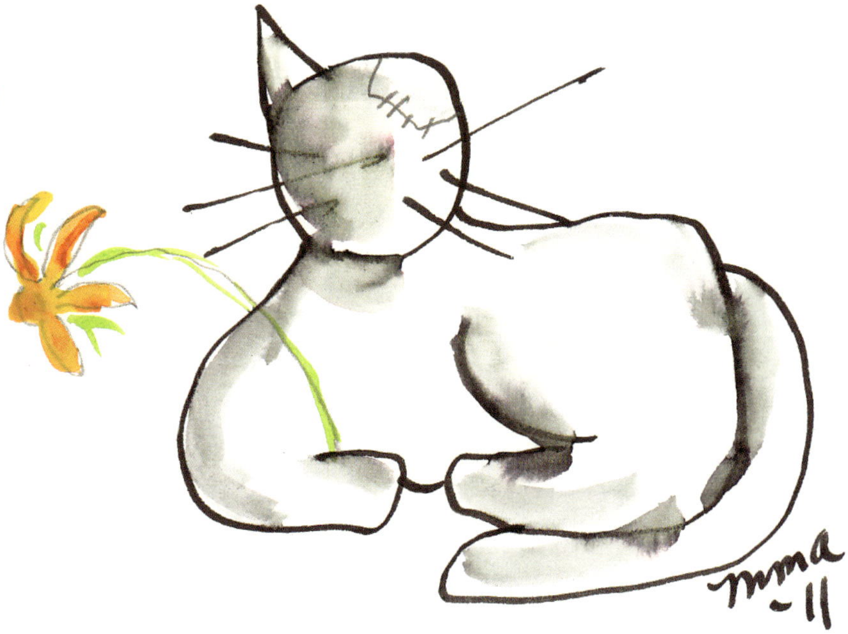

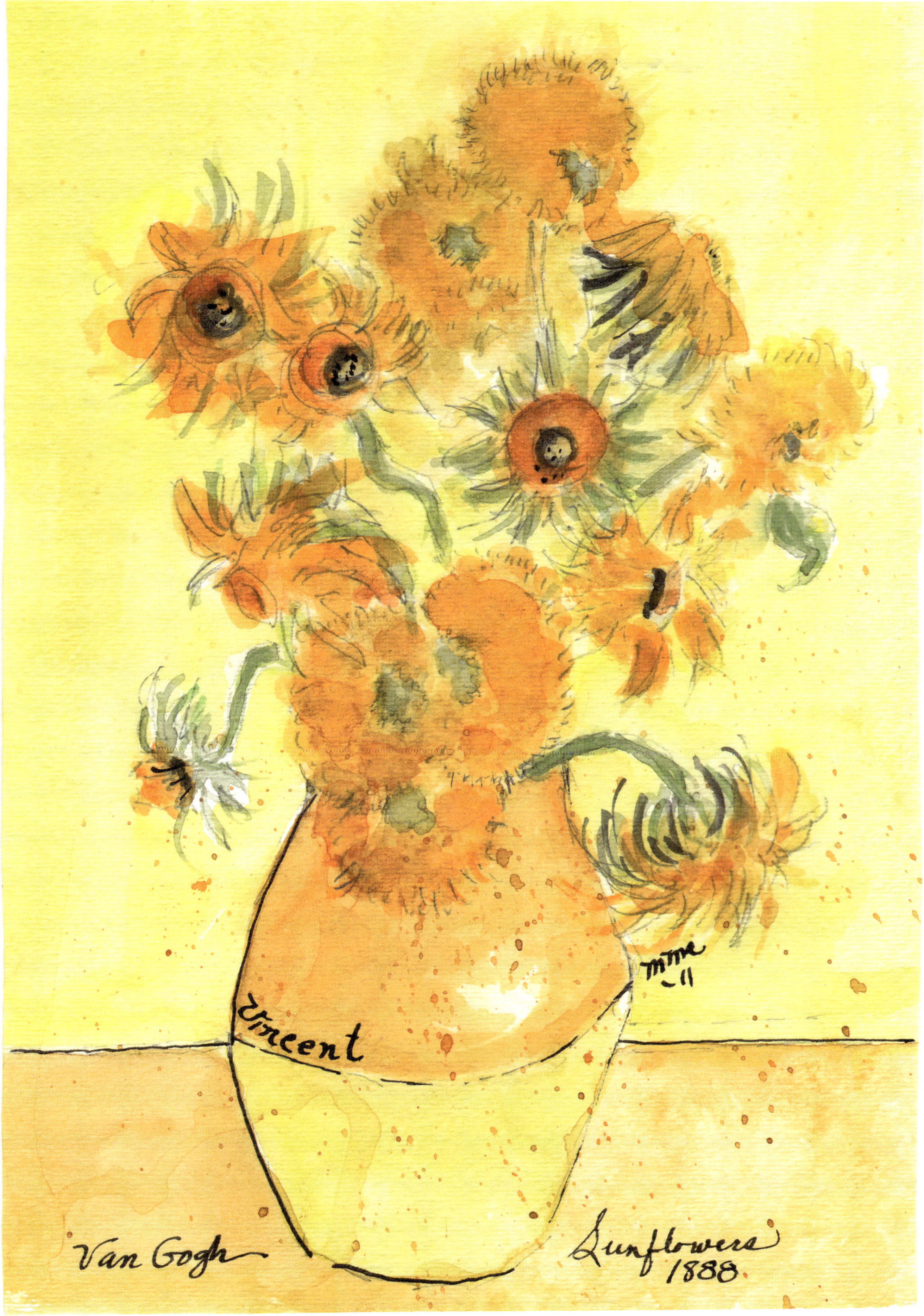
Vincent
mmc
-11
Van Gogh
Sunflowers
1888

Chagall's Cat

Chagall's cat was mystic
never realistic
it seems she's a dream
a fairy queen
in a mythical scene
and
it is noted
she floated
in air
sans care
without a trace
of haste
in her flight
just delight
and love
as she hovered above
with hope in her eyes
while she sailed
through the skies
like a whimsical wind
with a rooster
her friend.

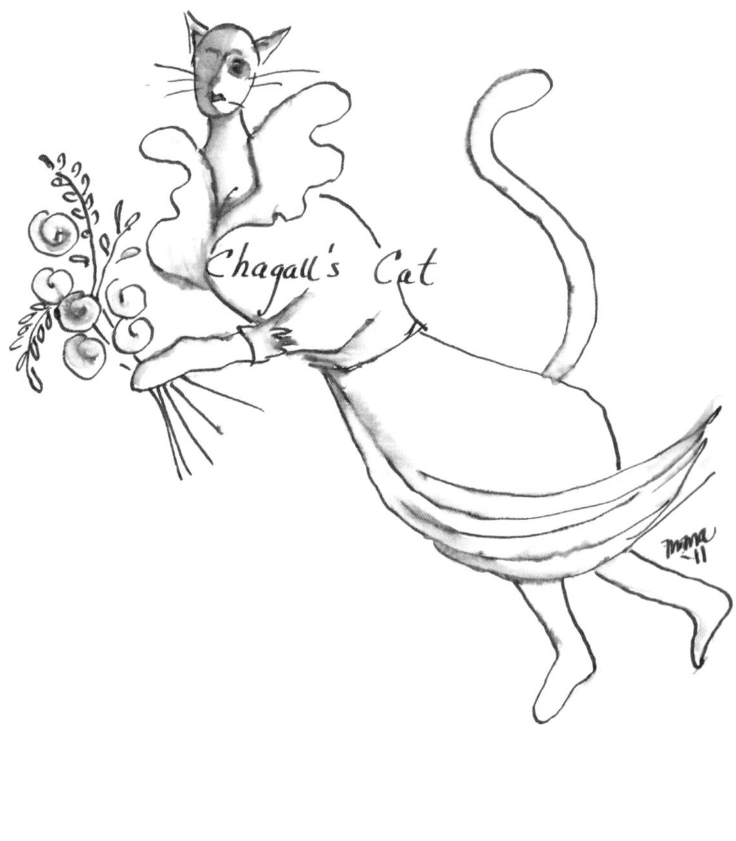

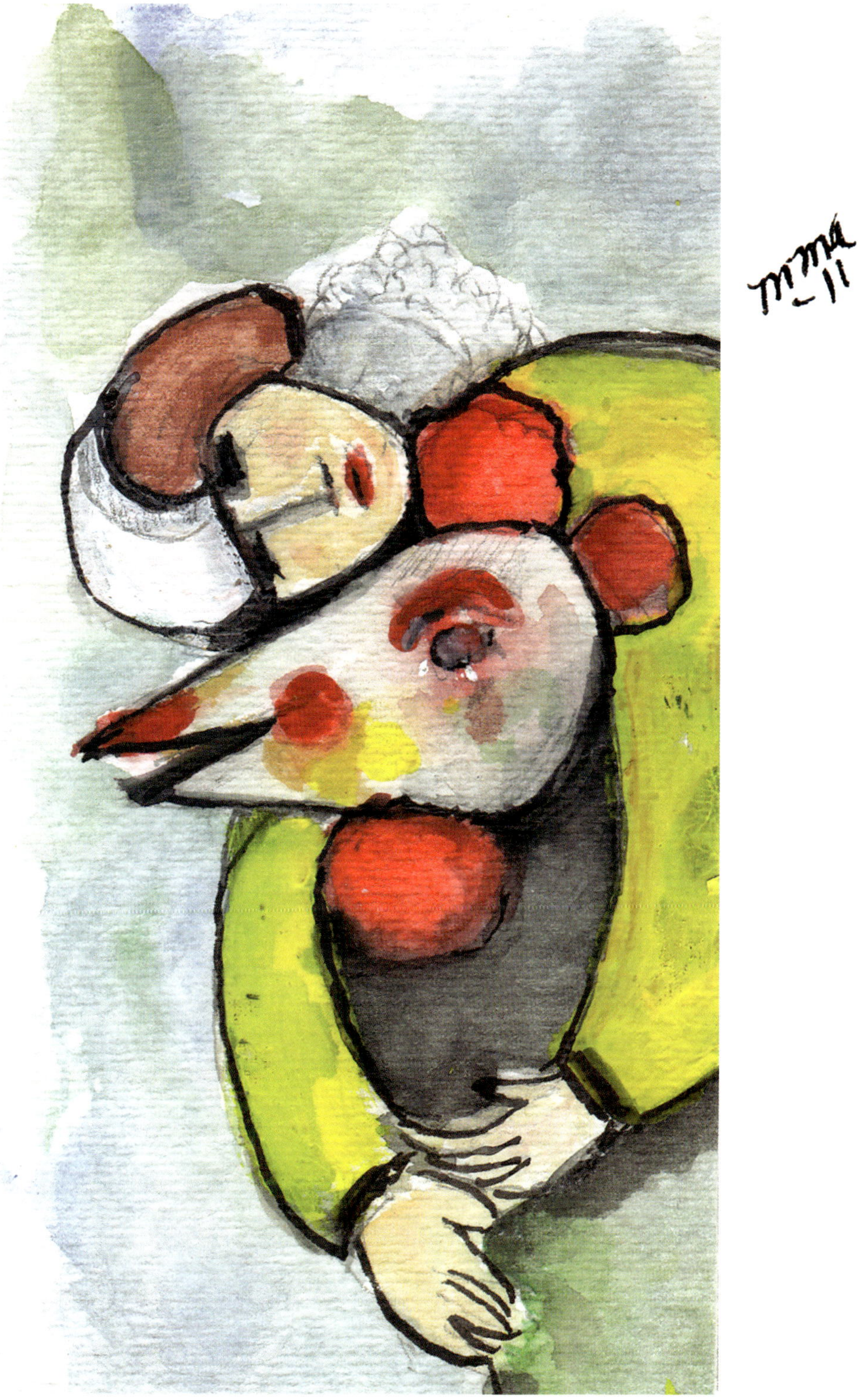

Marc Chagall
1928

The
Rooster

Monet's Cat
was
NOT
fond
of those
lilies
in the pond
so neath a
tree
in Giverny
one day
he expired
sick
and
tired
of Claude Monet